Mindful Emotions Workbook

A CBT Guide for Kids

2 FREE Bonuses!

Receive a **FREE** Planner for Kids and a copy of the Positive Discipline Playbook by scanning below!

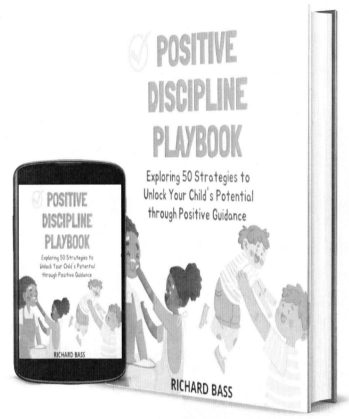

Contents

Introduction

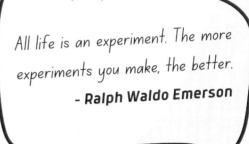

All life is an experiment. The more experiments you make, the better.

- Ralph Waldo Emerson

Meet Dani

Dani is an energetic middle schooler who loves telling jokes and practicing dance choreography with her friends. Her sunny personality and infectious laughter brighten every room that she steps into; nobody can resist her positive energy. School teachers describe Dani as the class *cheerleader*, while her friends describe her as the *Dance Queen*.

However, like many children her age, Dani struggles to regulate her emotions. Whenever she is feeling frustrated, her emotions become big and uncontrollable. Dani's big emotions can sometimes make it difficult for her to concentrate in the classroom, show kindness to her friends, or listen to her parents at home.

Recently, Dani's parents took her to cognitive behavioral therapy (CBT) sessions with a licensed therapist to teach her how to manage big emotions whenever she is stressed or anxious.

The therapist taught Dani tips on how to become a better problem-solver and communicator so she can get herself out of sticky situations and ask for help whenever she needs to.

The same skills and exercises that Dani learned during those therapy sessions have been incorporated into this workbook! Yes, that's right. *Mindful Emotions Workbook: A CBT Guide for Kids* is every middle schooler's secret weapon for learning how to identify, describe, and process difficult thoughts and emotions- without having to visit a therapist!

This practical, at-home, self-healing workbook is designed to help you develop the skills to confidently express big emotions without acting upon them, find ways to cool down and relax whenever you are feeling upset, and get into the habit of practicing positive social behaviors.

Throughout the next eight chapters, you will read more about Dani's personal challenges with regulating her emotions and observe how she reacts to different situations. At the end of each chapter, you will get to weigh in on how you would approach each situation if you were in her shoes.

Along the way, you will also get the opportunity to practice different types of CBT skills and exercises, such as mindfulness, emotional regulation, and cognitive restructuring skills. Having the knowledge and practice in these skills will help you courageously confront any problem, big or small, that may come your way!

> What you think of yourself is much more important than what others think of you.
> - Lucius Annaeus Seneca

What Is Cognitive Behavioral Therapy?

The exercises provided in this workbook are inspired by cognitive behavioral therapy, also called CBT. You may have heard about CBT from your family doctor, school counselor, or a classmate who has tried it before.

In a nutshell, *CBT* is "a type of psychotherapy that focuses on helping you understand and accept your thoughts and emotions. It is recommended for people who desire to learn how to replace negative thoughts or control big emotions."

CBT sessions are conducted by a licensed therapist. However, nowadays, it is common to find CBT exercises online that can be practiced from the comfort of your home. These exercises are valuable because they teach you how to cope with stress, reframe your thoughts, and calm yourself down when you are upset.

Furthermore, CBT exercises expose you to important skills you may not have learned from your parents or school teachers. Some of the skills taught include:

Emotional regulation: How to recognize, describe, and manage your emotions so you can avoid emotional outbursts.

Self-awareness: Learning about your thoughts, feelings, and attitudes and understanding how they impact your behaviors and interactions with other people.

Cognitive restructuring: Making adjustments to how you think or what you believe so you can see the world from a positive perspective.

Mindfulness: Noticing and embracing the present moment and accepting life as it comes without trying to change yourself or other people.

Behavior management: Identifying unhealthy behaviors and taking the necessary steps to develop new and improved habits.

How Does Cognitive Behavioral Therapy Work?

The main focus of CBT is to emphasize the relationship between your thoughts, emotions, and behaviors and how each factor contributes to another.

Your thoughts trigger specific emotional reactions, which motivate you to carry out specific behaviors. For example, if you think, I can't solve this math problem, which emotion are you likely to feel: excitement or frustration? That's right. Thinking that you can't solve a math problem will most likely cause you to feel frustrated.

Once you are frustrated, how are you likely to behave? Are you more likely to do a happy dance or sulk in your room? That's right. When you are frustrated, you are more likely to isolate yourself from the rest of your family.

CBT exercises are created to help you identify the connection between your thoughts, emotions, and behaviors. In particular, they help show you how unwanted thoughts trigger unwanted emotions and motivate unwanted behaviors. By adjusting your thoughts, you can successfully adjust your emotions and behaviors.

The Purpose of This Workbook

This CBT-inspired workbook has been created to help you learn how to regulate your emotions, cope with stressful events, and develop positive social behaviors.

In each chapter, you will be given age-appropriate exercises to practice in the comfort of your own home and at your own pace. These exercises will come in handy when you are faced with overwhelming situations at school, at home, or within your friend group.

The overall goal of this workbook is to provide you with healthy coping skills to use whenever you have a problem to solve. Having a variety of healthy coping skills to choose from whenever problems arise can stop you from practicing behaviors such as yelling, overthinking, procrastinating, throwing tantrums, and getting into arguments with friends or family members.

How to Use This Workbook

Before you start going through the workbook chapters, here are a few things you need to know:

- The workbook consists of 8 chapters and 33 exercises in total. Each chapter explores a unique CBT skill and offers some exercises to practice.
- It isn't necessary to complete the chapters in numerical order (e.g., starting with Chapter 1, then 2, then 3). Feel free to randomly select chapters that interest you, or start with the ones that are most important in your life right now.
- Each chapter will begin with a short story about a problem that Dani-our middle schooler whom you met in the introduction-is confronted with. At the end of every chapter, you will get to weigh in on Dani's dilemma and make recommendations or state what you would do differently if you were in her shoes.
- You are welcome to complete the workbook with your parents; however, the exercises are simple and practical enough to complete on your own.
- Lastly, please note that the CBT-inspired exercises included in the workbook do not replace seeking professional medical assistance. If you are aware of any serious or ongoing emotional issues you may be dealing with, it is important to speak with an adult or a therapist before completing the workbook.

Now that you know what to expect and how to work through the workbook, it is time to begin!

Chapter 2 Identify Unwanted Thoughts

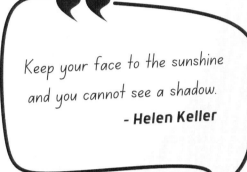

Keep your face to the sunshine and you cannot see a shadow.
- Helen Keller

The Day Before the Math Test

Dani took two big sighs and cupped her head in her hands as she leaned over her math textbook, trying desperately to focus on completing a few more word problems. It was the day before a big math test, and her anxious thoughts had begun spiraling out of control.

She gleaned at the numbers on the page, but suddenly, nothing was making sense. "How could I forget everything I have been studying so hard for?" she cried. Her mind was racing with all kinds of unwanted thoughts, like what would happen if she went blank during the test? And, as a result, failed the test?

Dani envisioned herself performing poorly on the test, getting yelled at by her math teacher in front of the entire class, and other extreme and embarrassing situations that could happen on the day of the math test.

With each unwanted thought, her self-confidence dropped lower and lower until she eventually didn't believe it was possible to pass the test.

What Are Unwanted Thoughts?

Have you ever experienced bizarre, awkward, or upsetting thoughts that randomly come into your mind? These thoughts are known as unwanted thoughts because of how they interrupt your normal thinking pattern and make suggestions that are harmful, unkind, or inappropriate.

Unwanted thoughts are a type of negative thinking that cannot be prevented. As scary or strange as these thoughts can sometimes be, there is no way to stop your mind from allowing them inside your head. It may also seem like the more you try and ignore or get rid of the thought, the more powerful it becomes in your mind. Experiencing unwanted thoughts isn't unusual. Research from the Anxiety and Depression Association of America shows that over six million Americans are affected by unwanted thoughts (Bilodeau, 2021).

Moreover, you are more likely to experience these types of thoughts whenever you are feeling stressed about something. They may either last for a short period until your stress subsides, or they may continue for a few days, depending on what kind of stressful situation you are facing. Some of the physical symptoms that occur whenever unwanted thoughts arise include:

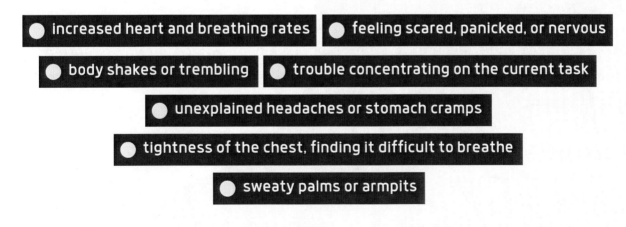

- increased heart and breathing rates
- feeling scared, panicked, or nervous
- body shakes or trembling
- trouble concentrating on the current task
- unexplained headaches or stomach cramps
- tightness of the chest, finding it difficult to breathe
- sweaty palms or armpits

Unwanted thoughts can sometimes appear as a small voice inside your head, making nasty comments about you or other people, encouraging you to make bad choices, or describing the worst-case scenarios.

Have you ever encountered this small voice inside your head? Can you remember some of the bizarre or hurtful things it has said to you? Write some of them down.

_____

_____

_____

_____

_____

_____

Labeling Unwanted Thoughts

Take a moment and think about what you normally do whenever you experience an unwanted thought. Does your approach help to make you feel better, or do you end up feeling worse?

Since unwanted thoughts are so frightening or inappropriate, you might address them in the following ways:

- Believe that the thought is real and feel upset.

- Pretend that the thought doesn't exist and block it out.

- Explore the thought deeper and discover more frightening ideas.

All of the examples mentioned above can make unwanted thoughts stay longer than they need to in your mind. In some cases, you may get tricked into believing that the thought is how you feel about a situation when, in reality, it isn't.

The best way to free yourself from unwanted thoughts is to label them and remind yourself that they are random and not controlled by you. This will allow you to continue whatever task you were busy with before the thought entered your mind, and authorize it to naturally drift away in its own time.

In other words, labeling and accepting unwanted thoughts helps you feel comfortable having them float in your head without giving them any attention. Instead of overreacting whenever they arise, you can simply notice what type of thought you are having (e.g., say to yourself, "I am having an unwanted thought"), take a few deep breaths, and get back to the task you were focusing on.

Exercise 1: *Label Your Unwanted Thoughts*

Unwanted thoughts come in all shapes and sizes. Some are big and hairy, while others are subtle and sneaky. Here are seven common types of unwanted thoughts that you may encounter. For each type, provide a real-life example of a situation when the unwanted thought can appear.

1. Unreasonable fear

Unreasonable fear occurs whenever your anxiety or panic is larger than the actual problem you are faced with. This can lead to overreacting or jumping to the worst conclusions, such as thinking, *I will fail the grade!*

Write down a real-life example of when you might experience unreasonable fear.

_____

_____

_____

_____

_____

2. Obsessive thinking

Obsessive thinking occurs when you spend hours or days worrying about the same situation, thinking about how it might unfold. You may notice a cycle of repeating the same negative thoughts in your mind and finding it difficult to move past the situation.

Write down a real-life example of when you might experience obsessive thinking.

_____

_____

_____

_____

_____

3. Unwanted images

Unwanted mental images appear when you see flashbacks of a painful memory or visualize a scary scenario happening to you or someone you care about. These images can seem very real, even though they are created in your mind.

Write down a real-life example of when you might experience unwanted images.

_____

_____

_____

_____

_____

_____

4. Self-criticism

Self-criticism occurs whenever you hear that small voice inside your head repeating nasty and unkind comments about you. The voice acts like a bully, constantly looking for new ways to pull you down and make you question your decisions.

Write down a real-life example of when you might experience self-criticism.

_____

_____

_____

_____

_____

5. Perfectionism

Perfectionism arises when you aim for extremely high standards or results that are impossible to reach. Creating and aiming for these high standards can make you feel anxious, especially when you aren't able to achieve them. In addition, that small voice inside your head can make you feel bad for not accomplishing the goals you had set for yourself.

Write down a real-life example of when you might experience perfectionism.

_____

_____

_____

_____

_____

6. Comparisons

Comparisons occur when you score your abilities, performance, or possessions against somebody else's. These types of thoughts cause you to think of yourself as being better or worse than other people. The danger with comparisons is that you forget that you are unique and have different strengths and weaknesses from others.

Write down a real-life example of when you might experience comparisons.

_____

_____

_____

_____

_____

7. Self-sabotage

Self-sabotage happens when you act on a thought to do something that hurts you in the end. The action may seem fun or harmless at first, but carries serious consequences. Examples of self-sabotage would be acting on thoughts to skip class, lying about your whereabouts, or leaving an assignment until the last minute.

Write down a real-life example of when you might have thoughts that lead to self-sabotage.

_____

_____

_____

_____

_____

_____

_____

_____

What to Do the Next Time You Have Unwanted Thoughts

There is no way to avoid having unwanted thoughts because they come and go as they please. Practicing labeling and accepting your unwanted thoughts can make them feel less overwhelming whenever they appear. However, there is more that you can do to improve the way you respond to unwanted thoughts.

Exercise 2: *Proactive Coping Exercises to Manage Unwanted Thoughts*

You don't need to panic the next time you experience an unwanted thought. Here is a list of proactive exercises to manage unwanted thoughts. Find a quiet room or area in the house, so you can practice the strategies outlined below.

1. Pause, notice, and declare

Practice pausing, noticing, and declaring what you are experiencing. First, take a few deep breaths to calm your mind and give yourself a mental break. Second, try to identify what type of intrusive thought you are experiencing (e.g., is it unreasonable fear, obsessive thinking, unwanted images, etc.?). Lastly, declare out loud what is happening inside your head by saying something like, "I am experiencing obsessive thinking right now, and I will be okay."

Practice pausing, noticing, declaring, and sharing your experience. How did it go? What can you improve next time?

_____

_____

_____

_____

_____

2. Reframe the unwanted thought

Unwanted thoughts usually highlight the worst of a situation and ignore the positives. The next time you experience an unwanted thought, practice reframing it to reflect the positive aspects of the situation. Instead of thinking, "What's the worst that can happen?" imagine the best-case scenario!

For example:

Unwanted thought: _"My friends will laugh at me when they see my new haircut."_
Best-case scenario: _"My friends will take some time to get used to my new haircut, but they will end up loving it because I love it!"_

17

Practice reframing an unwanted thought and share your experience. How did it go? What can you improve next time?

_____

_____

_____

_____

_____

3. Ground yourself in the present moment

Unwanted thoughts have a way of causing you to spend more time inside your head than enjoying your life. One of the ways to prevent this from happening is to practice grounding yourself in the present moment. Practice paying attention to what is happening around you rather than the thoughts flooding your mind.

Here is a grounding exercise to try the next time you notice an unwanted thought. Engage your five senses by completing the following task:

- Identify five things in your surroundings that you can see with your eyes.
- Identify four things in your surroundings that you can smell with your nose.
- Identify three things in your surroundings that you can hear with your ears.
- Identify two things in your surroundings that you can taste with your tongue.

Identify one thing in your surroundings that you can touch with your hands.

Share your experience in grounding yourself in the present moment. How did it go? What can you improve next time?

_____

_____

_____

_____

_____

_____

_____

_____

Have Your Say

At the beginning of the chapter, you read about Dani's challenge with unwanted thoughts, which caused a great amount of anxiety before her math test.

Now that you have learned more about unwanted thoughts, what do you think Dani should have done in that situation? Are there any exercises that you can recommend to her?

_____

_____

_____

_____

_____

_____

_____

_____

Chapter 3

Play the Role of a Detective

> Instead of worrying about what you cannot control, shift your energy to what you can create.
> - **Roy T. Bennet**

Lights, Camera, No Action

Dani spent her afternoons preparing for the upcoming audition for a school dance competition. She worked tirelessly to learn new dance moves and took days searching for the perfect song that would showcase her skills. A few weeks later, the names of the selected dancers were pinned on the school bulletin board, but Dani's name was not there. She didn't make the cut.

Time suddenly stood still. She froze in disbelief and stared at the list for several minutes, hoping that this was a prank and that the real list-which had her name written-would be taken out. Some of her friends who had made it into the dance competition were hugging each other and celebrating their achievements, but one friend in particular, Allison, noticed that Dani wasn't doing well and went over to her.

"Dani, I know how hard you practiced for the audition, and I'm sorry you didn't make it through to the competition," she said with concern. Dani lifted her head and forced a smile.

"Don't worry about it, Allison," she responded, "I guess I'm not a good dancer after all."

Allison, who shared the same passion for dance as Dani, shook her head vigorously and said, "That isn't true and you know it! You wouldn't be called the *Dance Queen* if you were not a talented dancer. Don't give up. You will get another opportunity to showcase your moves."

Thoughts Are Not Always True

A thought is an idea that enters your mind and seeks to help you make sense of your current situation. Its primary goal is to help you understand what is happening around you or inside of you (i.e., how you are feeling) so that you can take action.

Some thoughts are heavily influenced by your emotions and change depending on your mood. For example, if you are happy, you might think, *Wow, I am having such a great day at school! But on days when you are tired or irritable, you might think, School is so frustrating. I can't wait to leave!*

Other thoughts are influenced by past experiences-good or bad. For example, if you have a history of falling off a bicycle and getting serious injuries, the next time you see a bicycle, you might think, *I'm not getting on top of that bike because it's dangerous.* In reality, the bicycle isn't dangerous, but since you have several bad experiences with it, you are reluctant to ride it.

Since thoughts roam around in your head, it is normal to think that every idea you have represents the truth. For example, just because you think the new girl or boy in the classroom is unfriendly, you can easily believe your assumption is true. However, the more you get to know them, the more you find out that they are kind and talkative.

Not every idea that enters your mind represents the truth. Some ideas are so twisted and irrational (e.g., unwanted thoughts) that they are so far removed from the truth! Part of your job in combatting negative thinking is to learn the difference between thoughts that are truthful, realistic, and based on facts and those that aren't. To do this, you will need to play the role of a detective!

What Is the Role of a Detective?

A crime cannot be solved without the trusted help of a detective. Their job is to look for evidence that might help police officers piece the puzzle of who committed the horrific crime.

The detective is a neutral person who doesn't formulate their own opinions about what might have happened. They rely on cold, hard facts to get to the bottom of the truth and pin down the correct suspects.

Playing the role of a detective can help you investigate thoughts before accepting them as the truth. Whenever a spontaneous thought pops up in your mind, you can take a neutral stance and look for evidence to see whether it is truthful, realistic, and based on facts or not.

Similar to a detective, you would ask yourself questions about the thought to test whether you should believe it or simply let it go. You will find that some negative thoughts are true, realistic, and based on facts.

For example, you might think that a certain movie is boring and a waste of your time. Based on your unique preferences, this negative thought could be true.

Perhaps you are not a fan of the movie genre, the actors who are starring in the film, or the general plotline. You can pull a lot of evidence to justify why you dislike the movie.

However, as a detective, there will also be times when you find that some negative thoughts are untrue, unrealistic, and not based on facts. For example, you might hear about a certain school that your parents are thinking of enrolling you at and think, *I hate that school. People there are weird.*

For this thought to be true, it would need to be realistic and based on facts. Some of the questions you might decide to ask yourself to examine the truthfulness of this thought could be:

- Have I visited the school before? If so, how was my experience?
- Do I know at least five people who attend the school? If so, are all five of them weird?
- Is my dislike for the school based on other people's opinions or my own?
- Could there be other underlying emotions behind my dislike for the school, such as fear or anxiety?
- Is my dislike for the school based on negative experiences I have had while visiting the campus?
- Can I list five facts about the people who attend the school that make them come across as weird?

The answers to these questions will help you decide whether it is safe to believe in the thought or not. If the thought passes your exam and you find that, indeed, the school is strange, then at least you have valid concerns to raise with your parents.

Detective Tools to Help You Challenge Negative Thoughts

Every detective needs a toolbox full of detective tools to assist them in completing their investigations. Whenever you are preparing to examine your thoughts and determine whether they are true or false, you will also need a set of detective tools to make the process run smoothly.

The following exercises will introduce you to some valuable tools to help you challenge negative thoughts. You will also get an opportunity to practice using the tool by reflecting on past negative thoughts.

Exercise 3: Questioning Your Assumptions

Assumptions are conclusions you draw about a situation when you don't have enough information available. Even though assumptions provide a shortcut, they aren't always truthful. Questioning assumptions involves asking open-ended questions that will help you come to an accurate conclusion.

Think back to a recent scenario where you assumed what was happening or what a person's behavior meant based on a lack of information. Write down the assumption you made below. For example, When my mother told me she needed time alone, I assumed she was upset with me.

Answer the following questions about your assumption to examine whether what you thought was true or not.

1. Is your assumption based on facts or feelings?

_____

_____

_____

_____

_____

2. What evidence is there that your assumption is true?

_____

_____

_____

_____

_____

3. What evidence is there that your assumption is false?

_____

_____

_____

_____

_____

4. Is your assumption fair? Does it consider both positive and negative aspects of the situation?

_____

_____

_____

_____

_____

5. If you told this assumption to a friend, would they agree with you?

_____

_____

_____

_____

_____

_____

Exercise 4: *Weighing the Consequences*

As we have already discussed, thoughts trigger specific emotions, which ultimately motivate specific behaviors. Thus, every thought has a positive or negative outcome. When examining negative thoughts, it is important to consider the consequences of entertaining those ideas.

Think back to a recent time when you experienced an unwanted thought-refer to the previous chapter to refresh your memory on unwanted thoughts. Imagine that you believed the unwanted thought was true, and answer the following questions:

1. What is your outlook on the world since believing that your unwanted thought is true?

_____

_____

_____

_____

_____

2. How have your relationships with friends and family changed since believing that your unwanted thought is true?

_____

_____

_____

_____

_____

_____

3.

How differently do you look at or think about yourself since believing that your unwanted thought is true?

_____

_____

_____

_____

_____

What challenges or limitations were created in your life since believing that?

_____

_____

_____

_____

_____

_____

4. How has your future been impacted since believing that your unwanted thought is true?

_____

_____

_____

_____

_____

_____

Exercise 5: *Coming up With Alternatives*

A good detective doesn't look at a crime scene at face value. He or she will explore alternatives about what might have happened to hopefully come closer to the truth. Similarly, whenever you are examining negative thoughts, consider alternative ideas that you may be overlooking. Ask yourself, "What other conclusions can I draw from this situation?"

Think back to a recent scenario where you were disappointed with the outcome of a situation and came to a negative conclusion, like thinking to yourself, *I am not smart enough.* Challenge yourself to come up with at least five alternative conclusions about that situation.

For example, instead of thinking, I am not smart enough, the alternatives could be:

- ○ I have a lot to learn
- ○ I am doing my best
- ○ I have my unique strengths
- ○ I can change what I can control
- ○ I am making progress

_____

_____

_____

_____

_____

_____

_____

_____

Have Your Say

At the beginning of the chapter, you read about how disappointed Dani was to learn that she hadn't made it into the dance competition. Her final remarks were, "I guess I'm not a good dancer after all."

Now that you have learned more about how to investigate and challenge negative thoughts, which two detective tools would you use to challenge your thoughts if you were in the same situation as her?

_____

_____

_____

_____

_____

_____

_____

_____

> Your emotions make you human. Even the unpleasant ones have a purpose. Don't lock them away. If you ignore them, they just get louder and angrier.
> — **Sabaa Tahir**

Nobody Understands Me

One evening, Dani and her parents sat down to an uncomfortable dinner at the table. It was obvious from the way Dani was pushing food around her plate and avoiding eye contact with her parents that she was upset about something, but nobody knew what the problem was.

Moments passed, and her mom decided to ask, "Dani, is everything okay?" Dani took a deep sigh and opened her mouth, but no words were coming out. Eventually, she stuttered a string of words, "I... I just feel... oh, never mind. You won't understand anyway."

Her parents exchanged glances, worried that there was more left unsaid by their daughter. However, they assumed she was having a bad day and would soon get back to her normal self.

At school the next day, Dani's English teacher, Miss Martin, gave the class an assignment. She asked them to write an essay about a special moment in their lives. Without hesitation, Dani knew she would write about going to her first dance class at the age of five. However, a few minutes into the assignment, she hit a roadblock: She struggled to describe the excitement of discovering a hobby that she loved.

Miss Martin noticed from the other side of the classroom that Dani was struggling to write. She went over to her desk and asked, "Dani, is everything okay?" Tears welled up in Dani's eyes as she looked up at her teacher. "I... I just feel... oh, never mind. You won't understand anyway."

"Sometimes we don't have the words to describe how we are feeling, Dani," said Miss Martin, "but that shouldn't stop you from trying. It takes time to learn how to express yourself, so cheer up. It will get easier."

What challenges or limitations were created in your life since believing that?

Back in kindergarten, you learned a handful of emotions that could describe how you are feeling at any given moment. Can you remember what some of these emotions were?

They may have included emotions like anger, fear, sadness, happiness, disgust, or surprise. These six emotions are known as primary emotions because they are the first you feel whenever an event takes place.

For the first few years of your life, these six emotions were enough to describe how different situations affected you. For example, when your parents would prevent you from playing outside, you would feel *angry*. When you were left in a classroom with new classmates, you would feel *scared*. Or when you were given a delicious serving of ice cream, you would feel *happy*.

As you have gotten older, your emotions have become more complicated than before, which has made it a lot harder to describe how you are feeling. For example, when you are having difficulty solving a math problem, *anger* isn't exactly the right word to describe how you are feeling. The more appropriate word to use would be *frustration*.

It is therefore important to broaden your understanding of emotions and learn about the hundreds of secondary emotions that can help you describe complex emotions with more accuracy. Secondary emotions are the multitude of variations that are created from primary emotions. In other words, each primary emotion can be expressed in a lot of different ways.

Consider the following table of primary and secondary emotions. Notice the different ways each primary emotion can be expressed.

Anger	Fear	Sadness	Happiness	Disgust	Surprised
Mad	Anxious	Lonely	Playful	Ashamed	Excited
Irritated	Nervous	Bored	Peaceful	Disappointed	Amazed
Annoyed	Scared	Rejected	Grateful	Disapproving	Shocked
Furious	Insecure	Guilty	Joyful	Hateful	Confused
Jealous	Threatened	Depressed	Proud	Awful	Energized

From the table, you can see how anger can be expressed as feeling >

- irritated
- Nervousmad
- furious
- jealous
- annoyed

Each of these secondary emotions describes a unique experience. For instance, some situations will make you feel annoyed, while others will bring out jealousy. Learning as many secondary emotions as you can will help you become a pro at expressing how you feel in different contexts.

Exercise 6: *Expand Your Emotions Vocabulary*

The best way to learn new secondary emotions is to whip out your dictionary and look up the definitions of the words. Look through the list and search for the definitions of the following secondary emotions, then use the emotion in a sentence, starting with the phrase: "I feel [secondary emotion] when..."

1. Nervous

_____

_____

_____

2. Amazed

3. Jealous

4. Peaceful

5. Awful

6. Guilty

7. Grateful

8. Excited

_____

_____

_____

_____

9. Lonely

_____

_____

_____

_____

_____

10. Energized

_____

_____

_____

_____

Exercise 7: *Feeling Opposite Emotions*

Another factor that complicates emotions is finding yourself in situations where you are feeling opposite emotions at the same time. Have you been in these types of situations before?

For instance, you may have felt excited about attending a new school because it was closer to your neighborhood but also anxious about the idea of making new friends. Excitement-a secondary emotion that comes from surprise-is the opposite of anxiety-a secondary emotion that comes from fear. However, both emotions are true and realistic.

Below are a few real-life scenarios where you might feel opposite emotions. Provide your own examples of two opposite emotions, using the statement: "I feel [first emotion], and also feel [second emotion] when..." Refer to the table of primary and secondary emotions for inspiration. Make sure that the emotions you select come from two different categories.

1. Scenario: Being instructed to do your household chores

_____

_____

_____

_____

_____

_____

2. **Scenario:** Getting an A+ for a test in a subject you find difficult

_____

_____

_____

_____

_____

3. **Scenario:** Getting to know the new kid in class

_____

_____

_____

_____

_____

4. Scenario: Receiving pocket money from your parents

_____

_____

_____

_____

_____

5. Scenario: Being told "No" when asking your parents for a favor

_____

_____

_____

_____

_____

How to Express Big Emotions With Clarity and Confidence

Telling your friends and family that you feel happy is easier than telling them you feel anxious, angry, or lonely. This is because big emotions like anger and fear can make you feel exposed and vulnerable.

It is common to feel speechless when you need to express big emotions to your parents or school teachers. Even though you might have an idea of how you are feeling, finding the courage to express those emotions can be tough!

Nevertheless, big emotions like anger or fear are just as important to share as light and positive emotions like happiness. The following exercises will guide you on how to express big emotions with clarity and confidence.

Exercise 8:   *Allow Yourself to Feel Unpleasant Emotions*

One of the factors that make it difficult to express big emotions is the idea that you are not allowed to feel certain emotions because they are *bad* or *wrong*. The truth, however, is that all emotions are equal and acceptable. Before you can express big emotions, you first need to allow yourself to feel them.

Close your eyes and imagine that your body is a house that welcomes every type of emotion, big or small, pleasant or unpleasant. Picture yourself opening the door to different types of emotions and making them feel accepted and valued.

For example, see yourself opening the door and greeting the *irritation* with a smile, saying, "Welcome irritation, make yourself at home!" Do this with several other types of emotions.

When there are no more emotions left outside, shut the door and sit down with all of the different emotions, which are your special guests. Give each emotion equal attention, listening to what they have to share with you. Make sure you don't ignore any emotion, even the big and scary ones-they need your kindness, too!

After you have completed the exercise, take a few minutes to share your experience. How did you enjoy the exercise? What did you learn about your emotions?

_____

_____

_____

_____

_____

_____

_____

_____

Exercise 9: *Take Ownership of How You Feel*

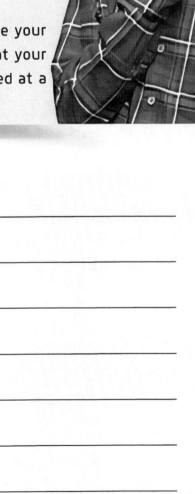

To ensure you are expressing emotions in a way that other people can understand, it is important to take ownership of how you feel. The aim is to make it very clear that this is an experience taking place inside of you.

A great way to show ownership of your feelings is to start with the words "I feel" whenever you are about to share your emotions. For example, "I feel upset when you call me nasty names" shows the other person how their habit of name-calling affects you.

Practice using "I feel [emotion] when" phrases to describe your emotions. Create three unique sentences; one directed at your parents, another directed at a friend, and another directed at a school teacher.

Exercise 10:   *Give Context Around Your Emotions*

It is also very helpful to share with others how your big emotions came about. For instance, what happened moments before you felt a specific way? Was there a specific behavior or experience that took place and caused your mood to change?

The following table provides a smart way to track how your emotions come about. Think of scenarios that would cause you to feel the emotions listed in the first column. Write down what happened moments before, as well as what happened moments after experiencing the emotion.

The first row has been completed for you.

Emotion	What caused the emotion?	What happened moments before?	What happened moments after?
Jealousy	I watched my sibling get a brand-new cell phone.	My parents walked in with a special gift for my sibling.	My sibling looked very happy, and I felt miserable inside.
Nervous			
Grateful			
Bored			
Proud			
Confused			

Exercise 11: *Be Upfront About What You Need*

Big emotions can reveal unmet needs that you would like others to respond to. For example, when you are annoyed with your parents, you might need them to do a better job at listening when you are speaking. Whenever you express big emotions, you can follow up by asking for what you need in order to feel better. This can also help the other person know what to do to support you.

Rewrite the statements you wrote in *Exercise* 9, adding on what you need others (i.e., your parents, friend, and school teacher) to do to help you. For example, "Mom, I feel bored when I sleep over at Grandpa's house. Next time, please, can I visit for the day and come back later with you?"

Step Into the Other Person's Shoes

Throughout this chapter, you have learned different ways to identify, describe, and express your emotions. However, another important skill you need to learn is how to understand other people's emotions. This is known as showing empathy.

One of the simplest ways to describe empathy is stepping into someone else's shoes and looking at the world-or the specific problem-from their perspective. To do this, you must put aside your own thoughts and feelings and pay attention to how the other person is feeling.

Empathy isn't about agreeing with the other person or feeling the same emotions as them; instead, it is about accepting that they can think and feel differently from you. For example, one of your friends can feel hurt by what you have said even though it wasn't your intention to hurt them. They may interpret your words in a way that makes them feel upset, which causes them to react differently from what you had expected.

The empathetic thing to do in this scenario would be to validate your friend's feelings and apologize for how you may have hurt them with your words. You might say something like, "I can see that you are offended by what I said. I am sorry for hurting you with my words. It wasn't my goal to do so."

Another way to practice empathy is to let go of seeking to be *right* in a conversation and instead focus on understanding where the other person is coming from. For example, if you are arguing with your parents, it is natural to feel the urge to defend yourself. However, this won't resolve the problem, will it?

For example, your parents may be frustrated with you for not completing your chores, and you may be frustrated with them for interrupting you at random times during the day to force you to do chores. Showing empathy toward them allows you to understand where they are coming from (i.e., they are angry because you won't do as they say) and think of a solution that would make both of you happy, such as creating a schedule for weekly chores, which fits around your routine.

The following exercises provide useful strategies to develop empathy for others.

Exercise 12:   *Assume the Best*

Typically, when you don't understand why someone is acting in a certain way, it is normal to jump to the worst conclusions. Nevertheless, being empathetic is about always assuming the best of people

For example, you might notice that your friend is acting differently toward you, maybe being less chatty. Instead of assuming they are mad at you (i.e., assuming the worst), you can assume they are just tired and prefer not to speak to conserve energy (i.e., assuming the best).

Think of five more recent scenarios where you didn't understand how your parents, siblings, friends, pets, classmates, or teachers were behaving. Write the scenarios down, stating the worst and best assumptions for each.

The first row has been done for you.

Scenario	Worst assumption	Best assumption
My friend didn't invite me to her house party.	This is a sign that my friend doesn't like me very much.	My friend cares for me. She simply doesn't have enough room in her house to accommodate all of the girls in the class. Next time, she will think of me.

Exercise 13:   *Find Similarities*

How you see the world is completely different from how your parents, siblings, friends, or teachers see it. Since each human being is unique, we all have a unique perspective. Nevertheless, there are a few ideas, values, or beliefs that we can agree on.

Showing empathy, especially to people who think and feel differently from you, is about looking for similarities you can both agree on. These similarities are what help you understand each other and find common ground.

For example, on the surface, you might think you don't have anything in common with a new student who has joined your class. But stepping into their shoes and seeing the world from their perspective allows you to find some similarities, such as:

- Both of you enjoy making jokes.
- Both of you wake up and go to school.
- Both of you are interested in the same hobbies.
- Both of you dislike homework.
- Both of you have goals that you are working on.

Think about two individuals in your life who think or behave very differently from you. In the space below, write down three to five similarities that you share with these individuals. You may need to ask them a few questions to find out more about their interests or personalities if you don't know them very well.

_____

_____

_____

_____

_____

Exercise 14: *Offer Validation*

Another great way to practice empathy is to validate how someone else may be feeling, even if you don't feel the same way. Offering validation doesn't require you to agree with the other person's point of view; it is about acknowledging what they are saying and allowing them to think or feel differently from you.

You can use different phrases to offer validation to others. For each phrase provided below, write a full sentence showing an example of how you would use the phrase in a real-life situation. Avoid adding your own opinions or beliefs.

1. I hear what you are saying.

_____

_____

_____

_____

2. What you are feeling is normal.

_____

_____

_____

_____

3. I am here for you.

_____

_____

_____

_____

_____

Have Your Say

At the beginning of the chapter, you read about how difficult it was for Dani to openly express what she was feeling. Now that you have a better understanding of how to describe and share your feelings, what advice would you give to Dani? How can she get over the fear of expressing her feelings?

_____

_____

_____

_____

_____

_____

_____

_____

_____

Chapter 5

Take a Powerful Pause and Breathe

> Practice the pause. Pause before judging. Pause before assuming. Pause before accusing. Pause whenever you're about to react harshly, and you'll avoid doing and saying things you'll later regret..
>
> **- Lori Deschene**

Reaching Boiling Point

It was a Saturday afternoon, and Dani was watching a movie on her table in the sitting room. She had waited all week to spend an hour and a half by herself, catching up on screen time. In the corner of her eye, she could see her baby brother approaching. He was a terrorizing three-year-old who caused a riot with his chunky toy trucks wherever he went.

"Reggie," she said sternly, "I feel annoyed when you play with your trucks while I am watching something. I need you to please turn around and play in your bedroom." Reggie grinned and proceeded to come closer, seeing an opportunity to place his trucks in the center of the coffee table, a few feet away from Dani.

"Reggie, I'm serious! Go away!" she said angrily. Meanwhile, Reggie was more interested in the various objects on the table, which could be mounted and used as part of his truck game.

It didn't occur to him how increasingly frustrated his sister was becoming.

Dani had no choice but to pause the movie, which sent her anger skyrocketing through the roof. Her heart was beating faster and faster as she approached her boiling point. In the background, she could hear Reggie imitating truck sounds, continuing like nothing happened.

Her emotions were bubbling to the surface and becoming increasingly difficult to hold back. She could feel the explosive reaction whirling inside, which would come out as a loud scream from the pit of her stomach. The poor three-year-old couldn't prepare for the monstrous rage that was moments away from being unleashed on him.

What Does It Mean to Pause?

To pause means to enjoy a break from taking action. For a brief moment, you stop whatever you are doing and freeze. However, taking a pause can also mean something completely different. When you are overwhelmed, taking a pause could mean enjoying a break from thinking or focusing on your emotions.

One of the reasons why emotions get bigger and bigger when you are upset is because most of your attention is directed at how you are feeling. The same applies to unwanted thoughts; they usually grow more powerful in your mind the more you think about them.

Taking a mental or emotional pause may be a great way to shift your attention away from the unpleasant thoughts or emotions you are feeling and enjoy some much-needed silence. In that moment of silence, you are able to take deep breaths, check in on yourself, and maybe even play the role of detective by challenging negative thoughts. This break is what you need to get your mind and body back to a normal state.

Here are a few more reasons why you should get into the habit of taking mental and emotional pauses:

- You get an opportunity to reflect on your current situation without fueling your emotions.
- You allow yourself to be present in the moment and embrace what is happening around you.
- You get to end the cycle of obsessive thinking and self-criticism and drown out the small voice inside your head.
- You are able to give your mind and body enough time to calm down and return to a normal and balanced state.

Finding Your Pause Button

An easy way to remind yourself to pause is to create a physical *pause button* somewhere on your body. Whenever you hit the button, it could be your cue to stop whatever you are doing, thinking, or feeling and take a few moments to breathe.

Your pause button should be an area of your body that is easily accessible and can be pinched to trigger your mind to stop thinking and focus on the present moment. Some ideas for pause buttons are your belly button, ear lobe, or the area of skin between your thumb and index finger.

Hitting the pause button should be something you do whenever you are feeling overwhelmed and can sense your thoughts getting darker and emotions becoming stronger and uncontrollable. Think of this button as an emergency break that brings everything to a screeching halt and allows you to calm down.

Some of the scenarios where you might need to hit the pause button include:

- arguments with friends and family
- feeling stressed before or during a school test
- engaging in unwanted thoughts, like talking down to yourself
- feeling misunderstood and seeking to defend yourself
- feeling angry and having the urge to say hurtful words

When any of these scenarios occur, find your pause button and press on it firmly. Continue to apply pressure on the button until your mind starts focusing on the physical discomfort rather than the spiraling thoughts or emotions you are experiencing. Eventually, your thoughts will gradually disappear, and the build-up of emotions you feel will become less intense.

While pressing your pause button, you can even say a few encouraging words to yourself, like:

- "Everything is going to be okay."
- "I am in control of my thoughts and feelings."
- "I am doing the best that I can."
- "I am proud of myself for calming down."
- "I am safe. I don't need to panic."

There is no rule for how long you should hold your pause button. What's important is to make sure that you are giving yourself enough time to breathe and relax while taking your pause.

Relaxation Techniques That Can Help You Pause

In addition to finding your pause button, a number of relaxation techniques can help you take a moment to calm down. What's great about these techniques is that they can be incorporated into your routine and become healthy habits you practice on a daily basis.

The following exercises will introduce each relaxation technique and provide simple instructions to get started.

Exercise 15: Deep Breathing

Deep breathing is the act of taking slow and full breaths that allow more oxygen to your brain, creating a pleasurable, relaxed feeling.

Typically, stress causes you to take irregular, short breaths that increase your heart and breathing rates and trigger a feeling of anxiety. To reverse this process, you can actively control your breathing by slowing it down and making each breath longer.

A simple deep breathing exercise that you can practice is known as box breathing. The aim is to make each inhale and exhale breath-as well as two pauses in between-the same length and breadth, creating an invisible box.

Below are the instructions:

1. Sit in a comfortable position with your hands resting on your lap.

2. Begin to inhale through your nose for three slow counts.

3. Pause and hold your breath for another three slow counts.

4. When you are ready to release your breath, exhale through your mouth for another three slow counts.

5. Complete the box by pausing and holding your breath for a final three slow counts.

Practice the box breathing exercise and share your thoughts below. How did the exercise go? What can you improve next time?

_____

_____

_____

_____

_____

Exercise 16: *Physical Exercise*

Another great way to relax is to move your body through physical exercise. Whenever you engage in an active sport or workout, your brain releases chemicals that fight against stress and cause you to feel confident and motivated.

Fortunately, your brain doesn't need intense physical exercise to release these chemicals. A moderate 10-minute physical activity that increases your heart rate and allows you to break a sweat is enough. If you already live an active lifestyle (e.g., you play school sports and spend most days outdoors), then you are in luck! But if not, you may need to find things to do around the house that keep you active.

Here are some uncommon activities that can help you stay active:

- walking your pet
- doing household chores
- watering garden plants
- helping your parents prepare meals
- cleaning your bedroom

There are also more traditional ways of staying fit, such as:

- playing tag
- riding your bicycle
- playing a sport
- swimming
- completing a workout tutorial

In the table provided, create a five-day physical activity plan that you can follow for one week. Under each day of the week, add at least one physical exercise for you to try.

Activity	Monday	Tuesday	Wednesday	Thursday	Friday
Physical exercise 1:					
Physical exercise 2:					
Physical exercise 3:					
Physical exercise 4:					
Physical exercise 5:					

Exercise 17: *Mindfulness*

Practicing mindfulness can be a relaxing way to pause and enjoy the present moment. So often, the things that worry you are not happening in real life but rather taking place inside your head.

Mindfulness encourages you to take a pause from thinking and focus on being alert to what is happening in real life. You may come to realize that your concerns are not as serious as your thoughts make them out to be.

A simple way to practice mindfulness is to notice the beauty of your surroundings. Stop thinking and take a moment to appreciate the small objects that make your space interesting. For example, notice the shape of the couch, the rich color of the cushion, or the size of the TV screen. These are objects that we can sometimes take for granted.

Another way to practice mindfulness is to notice or listen to the sensations occurring in your body without labeling or judging them. Flow with them, allowing them to grow or subside in their own time. Your job is to listen to the sensations like you would listen to a song. Stay tuned in until you feel relaxed and calm.

Practice both of the mindfulness exercises mentioned above and share your experience below. How did the exercises go? What did you learn?

_____

_____

_____

_____

_____

_____

Have Your Say

At the beginning of the chapter, you read about Dani's explosive interaction with her baby brother, Reggie. Now that you have a better understanding of how to pause and calm yourself down when you are stressed or overwhelmed, what advice would you give to Dani? What exercises would have helped her calm down during that heated encounter?

_____

_____

_____

_____

_____

_____

_____

_____

_____

Chapter 6 How to Solve Tough Problems

> There's no use talking about the problem unless you talk about the solution.
>
> **- Betty Williams**

My Dog Ate My Homework

After taking a short 10-minute break to stretch her legs outside, Dani returned to her bedroom to find her history assignment shredded into pieces on the floor. "Oh no," she desperately cried, "I shouldn't have left Brody inside my room!" Brody was her mischievous Labrador, who got excited whenever he saw papers. He must have discovered Dani's history assignment on her desk and clawed through it!

It was the day before the assignment deadline, and Dani didn't know how she would be able to complete a week's worth of work. She also didn't want to submit a chewed and glued-together assignment that her teacher couldn't read. Making excuses wouldn't help her get out of trouble, but neither would telling her history teacher that her dog ate her homework!

She pinched her ear lobes and took five minutes to pause and take deep breaths. "Breathe, Dani," she whispered to herself, "you will think of a solution. Everything will be okay."

What Is Problem-Solving?

According to the American Society for Quality, problem-solving can be defined as "the act of defining a problem; determining the cause of the problem; identifying, prioritizing, and selecting alternatives for a solution; and implementing a solution" (What is problem-solving?, 2021).

Based on this definition, we can see that problem-solving is a process that consists of three steps, which are:

Step One: *Define the Problem*

Before you can brainstorm solutions for a problem, you need to be clear about what you are trying to solve. Defining the problem involves looking back at the crisis at hand and identifying the main issue so you can be specific about what you are trying to fix.

Some questions that can help you define the problem are: What? Where? When? Who? Here is a brief breakdown of each question:

- **What:** What do you hope to achieve? What is the desired outcome that can help you solve the problem?

- **Where:** Is there a specific location where this change needs to take place?

- **When:** Is there a specific time when you need to have the answers or solutions?

- **Who:** Are there specific individuals who can help you arrive at the desired outcome who may need to be included in the problem-solving process?

Step Two: *Generate, Prioritize, and Select Options*

Problem-solving is sometimes referred to as a creative process because it considers a multitude of options for arriving at the desired outcome. Giving yourself options allows you to think out of the box and look for new and improved ways of addressing problems.

The best way to generate alternatives is to engage in a brainstorming exercise. Grab a pen and paper and write down every small or big possible solution that you can think of. Afterward, you can scrutinize each idea and narrow them down to the top five or ten that you like. You may even decide to combine two or more really good ideas and end up with three strong possible solutions.

The final step is to look at your options and select the main solution that you will test or carry out. Make sure that your main solution ticks the following boxes:

- The solution will effectively solve your problem without creating new problems.

- You can carry out the solution using materials or resources you already have.

- Every individual impacted by the problem is comfortable with you testing the solution.

Step Three: *Take Action and Gather Feedback*

Once you have come up with a solution, the only thing left to do is test it out. Be prepared to make mistakes or encounter challenges during this process. Mistakes and challenges are a part of your experimentation, making for valuable feedback.

After carrying out your solution, take notes about how the task went and how you can improve next time. For instance, were there unexpected loopholes that you will need to consider in the future? Did the task take longer than you expected?

If your solution isn't as successful as you would have hoped, don't be discouraged. Take the feedback and implement the changes to improve on the next try. Alternatively, revisit Step Two and test out another potential solution you have come up with.

Exercise 18: *Problem-Solving Skills Quiz*

Everybody has the potential to be an effective problem-solver. However, this is a skill that needs to be cultivated and nurtured over time.

Four skills determine how effective you are at solving problems, namely being able to sense, feel, think, and rely on your intuition. To test your problem-solving abilities, you can determine which skills you are mostly good at and which skills you need to improve on.

The following quiz tests your strength in the four problem-solving skills. Consider each statement—question—and circle the response that resonates with you most. You can pick one out of five responses:

● Strongly agree = 5 points

● Slightly agree = 4 points   ● Slightly disagree = 2 points

● Strongly disagree = 1 point   ● Not sure = 3 points

At the end of the quiz, you will add up the totals for each question and assess how well you performed at each skill—out of **25**.

Statement (Questions = Q)	Strongly agree	Slightly agree	Not sure	Slightly disagree	Strongly disagree
1. I am often told that I am a logical thinker.	5	4	3	2	1
2. I wear my heart on my sleeve; I am very sensitive.	5	4	3	2	1
3. My teachers would say I am a detail-orientated person; I like being meticulous with my work.	5	4	3	2	1
4. Most of my friends agree that I am an intelligent person.	5	4	3	2	1
5. I prefer to worry about problems that affect me right now than problems that will affect me in the future.	5	4	3	2	1

Statement (Questions = Q)	Strongly agree	Slightly agree	Not sure	Slightly disagree	Strongly disagree
6. I like to ensure everyone around me is happy and nobody is left out.	5	4	3	2	1
7. I find it difficult to solve a problem without having all the facts in front of me.	5	4	3	2	1
8. I like to focus on the big picture and get bored when I need to consider every small detail.	5	4	3	2	1
9. When working in a group, I enjoy my interactions with my team members more than tackling the task at hand.	5	4	3	2	1
10. I am motivated to solve a problem only when I understand what's in it for me.	5	4	3	2	1

Statement (Questions = Q)	Strongly agree	Slightly agree	Not sure	Slightly disagree	Strongly disagree
11. I can solve a problem in record-breaking time without procrastinating on the details.	5	4	3	2	1
12. When I need to make a tough decision, I do it. I don't care if other people are hurt in the process.	5	4	3	2	1
13. I get easily bored repeating the same routines or processes.	5	4	3	2	1
14. I can tell by looking at other people's faces how they feel about a decision.	5	4	3	2	1
15. I don't let problems stress me out, regardless of how serious they are.	5	4	3	2	1

Statement (Questions = Q)	Strongly agree	Slightly agree	Not sure	Slightly disagree	Strongly disagree
16. I don't like to step outside my comfort zone or experiment with ideas I haven't tested before.	5	4	3	2	1
17. It is important for me that my team members work together in harmony so we can avoid conflict.	5	4	3	2	1
18. New problems get me excited because I love the thrill of a new challenge!	5	4	3	2	1
19. I am a fast learner, but I don't like doing a lot of research to solve a problem.	5	4	3	2	1
20. I don't need people to agree with me to make a decision.	5	4	3	2	1

Calculate your scores:

Use the following table to add up the scores for each problem-solving skill. For example, the sum—total—for Sensing skills will be the scores for Questions 4, 5, 10, 16, and 19.

	Sensing skills	Feeling skills	Thinking skills	Intuitive skills
	Score for Q4	Score for Q2	Score for Q1	Score for Q3
	Score for Q5	Score for Q6	Score for Q7	Score for Q8
	Score for Q10	Score for Q9	Score for Q12	Score for Q11
	Score for Q16	Score for Q14	Score for Q15	Score for Q13
	Score for Q19	Score for Q17	Score for Q20	Score for Q18
Total for each (out of 25):				

Here's what scoring high on each skill means:

- **High sensing skills:** You prefer organized and standard rules for solving problems. The more details and information you have about the problem, the better!

- **High feeling skills:** You are sensitive to other people's feelings and dislike sharing bad news. Your decisions take into consideration how other people will feel. You avoid solutions that may lead to arguments.

- **High thinking skills:** You rely heavily on facts and patterns to come up with the best solutions. It is important for you that your decisions make sense and can be tested through experiments.

- **High intuitive skills:** You get excited when there are new problems to solve because it means being able to think outside the box! You get bored with details or facts and would rather spend your time brainstorming creative ideas.

Problem-Solving Techniques to Apply in Different Situations

Now that you have an idea about which problem-solving skills you score high in, you can start to build on the areas where you need more support. For example, if you already have high feeling skills but fairly low sensing skills, perhaps you can focus on exercises that can help you pay more attention to the small details.

The following exercises reinforce all four problem-solving skills. For each exercise, think about a unique problem that you have dealt with—make sure you pick a different problem for each exercise or use the same one if you can't think of any new ones—and follow the instructions.

Exercise 19: Draw a Diagram

Trying to make sense of problems in your head can be confusing, especially when you are faced with problems that involve several steps or people. Drawing a simple diagram to illustrate the situation can help you define the problem and see what you need to do to begin solving it.

Think of a recent problem that occurred at home or school. Draw a diagram of the problem to illustrate the what, where, when, and who.

_____

_____

_____

_____

_____

Exercise 20: *Break Down the Problem*

When you are confronted with large problems that will take several months to resolve, it may help to focus on breaking the problem apart into smaller issues, steps, or processes that you can tackle on a daily, weekly, or monthly basis.

Think about a recent problem at home or school, which seemed big and complex. Break the problem down into smaller issues, steps, or processes that you can work through.

_____

_____

_____

_____

_____

_____

_____

_____

Exercise 21: *Consider the Impossible*

When problem-solving, it is important to consider every option, even those that seem unlikely or impossible. To do this, you will need to remove the barriers holding you back from exploring the possibilities. For example, instead of telling yourself that an outcome can't or won't happen, pretend it can!

Think about a recent problem at home or school where the solutions seemed unlikely or impossible. Give yourself permission to explore those possibilities and pretend that they actually can happen!

_____

_____

_____

_____

_____

_____

_____

Exercise 22: *Work Backward*

Another way to solve a sticky problem is to start with the end in mind. Think about what you would like the desired outcome to be, then work backward to identify the steps you need to take to achieve it. This strategy can also help you brainstorm ideas relevant to your goal and ensure you create strong possible solutions.

Think about a recent problem that occurred at home or school. Write out what you would have liked the desired outcome to be, then work backward to consider the steps you could have taken to achieve your goal.

_____

_____

_____

_____

_____

_____

_____

Exercise 23: *Ask for Advice*

Just because you have a problem doesn't mean you need to solve it alone. Asking for advice can be a great way to gather ideas on how you can address the challenges you are facing. Plus, you get to see how somebody else views your situation, which could be interesting!

Identify at least five people in your life who can offer you good advice. These could be friends who always have encouraging words to share, family members who are older and wiser, or people within your community, like your school teachers or sports coaches, who can provide expert advice on a particular subject. Write their names down and mention what type of advice you are more likely to seek from them.

_____

_____

_____

_____

_____

_____

Have Your Say

At the beginning of the chapter, you read about Dani's awkward dilemma: Her dog ate her homework! Now that you have a better understanding of how to solve problems, what advice would you give to Dani? If you were in her shoes, how would you solve this problem?

_____

_____

_____

_____

_____

_____

_____

_____

_____

_____

Chapter 7

How to Become a Better Communicator

> To effectively communicate, we must realize that we are all different in the way we perceive the world and use this understanding as a guide to our communication with others.
>
> **– Anthony Robbins**

Learning to Listen to Others

Dani's technology teacher, Mr. Hubbard, assigned the class into small teams to complete an exciting digital group project. He decided to place students into teams with classmates they hadn't worked with before, a challenge Dani gladly accepted!

Before allowing the teams to huddle together and get started on the project, he called Dani aside. "Now, Dani," he calmly said, "I need you to practice listening to other team members and giving them a chance to share their ideas too, okay?"

Mr. Hubbard knew that Dani had difficulty communicating effectively in group projects. Her unbridled energy in group activities caused her to speak the longest, interrupt others while they were presenting their ideas, and insist that things needed to be done her way.

"Yes, Mr. Hubbard," she agreed, "I will try my best to listen. Do you have any tips that I can practice?" Mr. Hubbard scratched his head and took a few minutes to think about her question. He then pulled out a piece of paper and a pen and wrote down a few communication tips.

He extended his hand and passed the piece of paper to Dani. "Here you go, my classroom cheerleader!" he said with warmth in his voice, "Now go back to your team and make me proud!"

What Is Open Communication?

Open communication is an important skill that enables you to express ideas with others through verbal or nonverbal language. It can help you clearly and confidently share your thoughts and feelings in a way that other people can understand.

The benefit of open communication is that you are encouraged to listen to others as much as you would like to be listened to. Listening carefully to what others are saying can help you gather information about what they are thinking and feeling, and then use this information to improve your ideas and make the conversation interesting and productive.

Moreover, open communication is about seeking to understand where others are coming from and why they may think or feel the way they do. Instead of assuming that you already know what others are thinking or feeling, you can ask open-ended questions to gain more knowledge about their perspective.
For instance, you are more likely to lead conversations with curiosity, genuinely showing interest in what others have to say. Plus, since you will be doing as much listening as speaking, you can make others feel special and respected whenever they talk with you!

Staying Open Even When It Is Hard to Do So

As much as you would like to openly communicate with others, there are times when you will get it wrong. For example, instead of giving others a chance to speak and share their ideas freely, you might interrupt them or dominate the conversation.

Remembering to be an open communicator isn't an easy job, especially in moments when you feel attacked by others. When you feel attacked, it is normal to go into defense mode and seek to justify yourself.

However, even during those vulnerable moments, taking the time to listen to others can help you stay curious enough to gather information about what others are trying to communicate and how you could possibly solve the miscommunication problems you are having.

The following exercises will show you how to practice open communication during difficult situations.

Exercise 24: *Separate Facts From Fiction*

Defensive behavior refers to standing by what you have said or done, even when your words or actions have been proven to be unacceptable or have hurt others.

To avoid defensive behavior, you can practice separating facts from fiction (i.e., what is true and false about what the other person is communicating) and taking responsibility for what is true.

Scenario: Your mother enters your bedroom and starts yelling about the dirty dishes left in the sink-which you were supposed to have washed. She continues to lecture you about how you never do anything around the house, which is an exaggeration because there are a few chores that you do around the house.

Write down three different ways to respond to your mother without being defensive. Start by separating facts from fiction and taking responsibility for what is true (e.g., "Mom, I hear you, and I am sorry for leaving the dirty dishes in the sink. However, I don't think it's fair to say that I don't do anything around the house.").

_____

_____

_____

_____

_____

_____

_____

Exercise 25: *Pick Your Words Wisely*

It is never a good idea to send a text or try and squash an argument when you are angry. Words come out of your mouth like toothpaste squeezed out of a tube-once you have said something nasty, you can't take it back.

Scenario: You hear a rumor that one of your friends has been gossiping about you behind your back. During break time, you get the chance to confront them about the rumor.

Suggest three ways to approach this discussion while practicing open communication. Your suggestions should show curiosity, include open-ended questions, and genuinely seek to understand the other person (e.g., "Allison, I heard something that bothered me yesterday, and I would like to bring it up with you. Is that okay?").

_____

_____

_____

_____

_____

_____

Exercise 26: *Ask for a Time-Out*

When your emotions take over, and you find it difficult to listen to what someone else might be saying, it is okay to ask for a time-out, a moment to pause and calm yourself down. This will help you avoid saying inappropriate words, taking unkind actions, or activating defense mode.

Scenario: You approach your teacher to discuss a low grade that you got for a test. According to you, the marking of the test was unfair, and you should have received a higher grade. But your teacher doesn't agree with what you are saying. The conversation becomes heated, and your voice starts to increase.

Provide three suggestions on how to ask for a time-out (e.g., "Sir, may I please take a few minutes to calm down outside?").

Exercise 27: *Meet in the Middle*

Seeking to always get your way in conversations can make it difficult to
understand and respect other people's needs. When others disagree
with you, it is because they have a unique way of looking at the
situation. Showing curiosity and asking questions allow you to find
similarities and meet in the middle so that everyone can walk away
feeling like a winner!

Scenario: You and a few friends disagree on which takeout
restaurant to order food from. Each person wants something
different, and this has made it difficult to come to a decision.

Write down three different ways to reach a compromise with your
friends and meet in the middle (e.g., "How about we order one
item from each restaurant and share the meals?").

_____

_____

_____

_____

_____

_____

Sharpen Your Listening Skills

A crucial aspect of open communication is knowing how to be a good listener. This involves paying attention to what others are saying and seeking to understand their message.

Take a moment and think about how easy or difficult you find paying attention to others when they are speaking. Do you often get distracted by your thoughts? Or do you feel an urge to finish their sentences or defend your point of view?

Patiently waiting for others to complete their messages can be hard, especially when you have a lot to say. However, it is the only way to make sure that everybody participating in the conversation has equal opportunities to speak and be heard. In group settings, in particular, listening to others shows how much you respect each individual's unique ideas, and this can lead to better collaboration and problem-solving.

Some ways to sharpen your listening skills include:

- **Look directly at the person speaking and nod to show that you are paying attention to what is being shared.**

- **Observe the speaker's body language to look for signs about how they may be feeling. For example, somebody crossing their arms and squinting their eyebrows or pointing their fingers may be frustrated.**

- **Take five seconds to pause before replying to the speaker so that you have a few seconds to process what you have heard and organize your thoughts.**

The following exercises provide additional support to help you build or enhance your listening skills.

Exercise 28:   *Show That You Are Listening*

Paying attention to the speaker means giving your full focus to what they are saying. This cannot happen when there are physical or mental distractions popping up.

Physical distractions include actions or objects within your environment that catch your eye and cause you to lose focus on the speaker. These could include things like:

● technological devices   ● people passing by

● sounds in the background   ● bright lights that are blinding

● action that seems more exciting

Sometimes, you may be caught off guard by mental distractions, which are thoughts that arise in your mind and create mental noise. These could include your own strong opinions, judgments, or criticism related to the message you are listening to.

Put together a plan on how you will avoid physical and mental distractions. Provide at least five action steps you can take to limit distractions. For example, you can put your cell phone on silent during group discussions to avoid being distracted by notification alerts.

_____

_____

_____

Exercise 29: *Reflect Back on What You Hear*

To make sure what you have heard is accurate, it is crucial to repeat the message back to the speaker. Allow them to clarify the message or confirm that you have heard it correctly. This should be done before you respond with your thoughts.

A good way to practice reflecting on what you have heard is to watch a TV show and pause whenever a character is done speaking, then summarize the main points they have made. Start with a phrase like, "What I hear you saying is..." and end with a question like, "Is that correct?" to give the speaker a chance to clarify their message. For example, "What I hear you saying is that you don't think the font we have chosen for the heading is the correct style. Is that correct?"

After you have practiced the exercise, share your comments below about how it went. What could you improve next time?

_____

_____

_____

_____

_____

_____

Have Your Say

At the beginning of the chapter, you read about Dani's trouble listening to others in group projects. Now that you have a better understanding of how open communication works, and the importance of listening, what tips would you give to Dani?

_____

_____

_____

_____

_____

_____

_____

> Needing help doesn't have a look, but asking for it always looks beautiful.
>
> -Brittany Burgunder

A Chat With the School Counselor

It was nearing the end of the school year, and Dani wasn't feeling like a normal self. On the outside, nothing seemed wrong. She was meeting her assignment deadlines, attending dance practices, and getting along with her friends. However, deep inside, she felt sad.

For a few weeks, Dani went back and forth in her mind about whether to seek help or not. She downplayed her sadness and thought other students needed support more than she did. But the feeling of sadness was persistent, day in and day out until eventually she summoned the courage to arrange a video call meeting with her school counselor.

When the day arrived for the meeting, Dani sat at her study desk with a pen and notebook, full of thoughts that she wanted to share with the school counselor and some burning questions she wanted to ask.

She took a deep breath and joined the meeting. On the other side of the screen was Miss Marshall, the school counselor, a gentle and soft-spoken woman who instantly put Dani at ease.

"Greetings, Dani!" said Miss Marshall, with a cheerful tone of voice, "How can I help you today?" Dani took a few seconds to gather her thoughts and feelings. Even though she didn't know what was causing her sadness, she wanted to express herself clearly and confidently.

"Greetings, Miss Marshall," she responded, "I haven't been feeling like my normal self lately, and it's starting to worry me. I have a few thoughts and questions to share with you. Maybe we can start there?" Miss Marshall seemed pleased with Dani's level of preparation for the meeting. For the next 30 minutes, she listened as Dani poured her heart out, bringing up different situations that were weighing heavily on her mind.

Miss Marshall thanked Dani for being courageous enough to seek help and promised that over the next few counseling sessions, they would address every issue raised and find healthy ways to cope. Dani was excited about continuing the sessions with Miss Marshall and believed that, over time, she would feel better.

Signs That You Are Not Coping

If you have ever felt an unshakeable and unexplainable sadness or hopelessness, you are not alone. Within the past decade, there has been a rise in mental health problems in young people.

You might be able to pinpoint where your stress or anxiety comes from. Some of the root causes might be:

- school pressure
- cyberbullying
- sounds in the background
- social isolation due to COVID
- ongoing family and household conflict
- pressure to look good
- school bullying
- social issues like community violence or natural disasters

In some cases, you cannot tell what the specific causes of your discomfort are; perhaps there isn't a major issue in your life that would cause you to feel sad, lonely, or stressed. Yet, deep inside, you feel unhappy and the sense that something is wrong.

It is substantial to understand that you don't need to be experiencing problems to feel sad. Sometimes, the feeling of sadness could flood your body for no good reason. Nevertheless, this doesn't mean that you should ignore the sadness. From a psychological perspective, feeling upset or *not like your normal self* for several weeks is a sign that you are not coping with the current tasks or events in your life, and it is time to seek help.

Exercise 30: *Signs You Are Not Coping Checklist*

You don't need to wait until you encounter a serious problem before you seek help. The earlier you can identify signs that you are not coping, the sooner you can address the underlying emotional issues and get back to your normal self.

The following table presents common warning signs that something is wrong and that you may need to seek help. Tick Yes or No for each statement. If you get five or more Yeses, consider speaking to someone about the symptoms you are experiencing.

Statement	Yes	No
1. I frequently lash out at other people without an explanation.		
2. I get extremely irritated at small things people do or say.		
3. I have picked up bad habits lately that help me zone out from the world.		
4. I tend to avoid problems by pretending they don't exist.		
5. When others seek to give me advice, I become defensive or emotionally shut down.		

6. I find it difficult to concentrate on tasks or remember important information.		
7. I have lost interest in hobbies that I used to enjoy.		
8. I feel exhausted most of the time, even though I get sufficient sleep.		
9. I dislike being around people and prefer to spend time alone.		
10. I have moments when I feel like crying without a good reason.		
11. I feel mad at myself for not being good enough.		
12. In recent months, I have put on a lot of weight or have lost a lot of weight.		

13. I have moments when I suddenly panic or feel restless.		

Reasons Why Asking for Help Is a Sign of Strength

One of the reasons why asking for help can be tough is how it is seen as a sign of weakness. For instance, you might think that your teachers will judge you for asking for additional class support or that your parents will be disappointed if you confess that you are feeling stressed and not coping with school demands.

The truth, however, is that asking for help requires a great amount of courage, which makes it one of the hardest but most admirable decisions you can make. When you ask for help, you are admitting that you are lost and need some guidance. While this can be an uncomfortable feeling, in exchange, you get to learn something new and improve your performance.

Part of growing up involves facing situations you haven't experienced in the past, such as puberty, peer pressure, or increasing responsibilities on your shoulders. It is, therefore, normal, and even expected, for you to frequently feel lost and confused. The benefit of asking for help is that you can receive the answers you need as quickly as possible to avoid staying in a state of confusion for months or years.

Asking for help immediately also means that you can learn what is acceptable and unacceptable and avoid repeating the same mistakes over and over.

The support you get from others can additionally reveal your strengths and weaknesses, allowing you to work on areas of your life where you struggle the most.

Overall, getting into the habit of asking for help makes you stronger than you were before. Not only can you improve your performance, but you can also build a stronger character and learn how to make good choices for your life!

Can you think of another benefit for asking for help that wasn't mentioned in this section? Write it down.

_____

_____

_____

_____

_____

_____

Building and Strengthening Your Social Support

Building and strengthening social support is essential for enhancing your well-being and making sure you have more than one person to turn to when you need help. Social support is defined as a network of people who can share information, offer advice, or support you in practical ways, like giving you food, shelter, or money when you need it.

The best part is that you don't need to be close with every person you turn to for help; however, there must be a foundation of trust between you. For example, you may not know every teacher personally, but being friendly in your interactions can help you build trust. Having a foundation of trust with the people in your social support system allows you to feel comfortable and confident seeking help in times of need.

The following exercises will help you brainstorm and identify people who you can add as part of your social support system.

Exercise 31:   Finding People Who Can Offer Emotional Support

Emotional support is the ability to show empathy and compassion toward someone when they are faced with challenges. There will be times when you are confronted with problems and need someone-or a few people-to provide you with emotional support. These could be people you know (i.e., your friends and family) or professionals trained to offer emotional support (i.e., a school counselor or licensed therapist).

Identify at least three people who have offered you emotional support in recent months or who you believe are capable of providing emotional support whenever you need it. Send each person a text during the week to inform them that they are part of your social support system.

The following exercises will help you brainstorm and identify people who you can add as part of your social support system.

Hey, Aunt Pam, I hope you are well. I just wanted to let you know that I have selected you to be part of my social support system. I will be reaching out to you when I need emotional support. Thank you for always being there for me during hard times.

_____

_____

_____

_____

_____

_____

_____

Exercise 32: *Finding People Who Can Help You Solve Problems*

There are some problems that you can confidently solve on your own and others that are complicated and require assistance from others. Having one or more people you can reach out to whenever you are faced with big and hairy problems can help you reduce stress when crises arise.

Identify at least three people who you can turn to when problems arise. Once again, these people don't need to be close friends or family members. They can be school teachers, sports coaches, or people you know from the community.

Keep in mind that each person needs to have experience solving the type of problems you are encountering. For example, your math teacher would be the best person to reach out to when you are having math-related challenges. Your older teenage sibling or cousin would be the best person to reach out to when you are having preteen or teenage challenges.

Similar to the instruction above, send each person a text and let them know that you have chosen them to be a part of your social support system and will reach out whenever you are faced with a specific problem. Feel free to use the lines below to draft your message.

_____

_____

_____

_____

_____

_____

_____

_____

_____

Exercise 33: *Finding People Who Can Offer Practical Support*

As a middle schooler who is on the cusp of entering high school and transitioning into adolescence, there are plenty of practical skills that you will need to learn. Some of these skills include:

● **how to study effectively**

● **how to make friends**   ● **how to manage money**

● **how to set and achieve goals**   ● **how to drive a car**

Unfortunately, many of these skills cannot be learned through watching YouTube tutorials; they can only be taught in person by dedicated loved ones, mentors, coaches, or professionals. Similar to the exercises above, identify at least three people who can teach you practical skills.

Choose people who you find it easy to learn from (e.g., they have a simple way of sharing information). In addition, you can look for people who possess certain qualities of good teachers, like patience, kindness, and wisdom.

Send each person a text during the week, informing them that they have been chosen to be a part of your social support system, and you will reach out when you need assistance learning specific practical skills. Use the lines below to draft your message.

_____

_____

_____

_____

_____

_____

Conclusion

CBT helps people understand their problems and create solutions by looking at the interaction between their thoughts (cognitions), emotions, behaviors, and physiology.

-Katie d'Ath & Rob Willson

Throughout this workbook, you have practiced several different types of CBT skills, which have exposed you to better ways of coping with stress and anxiety. In a nutshell, that is what CBT is all about-providing you with effective tools to respond to stressful situations in positive and healthy ways.

You are never too young to start practicing CBT and developing new habits that can enhance your quality of life and improve your relationships with others. If you have enjoyed the exercises you have learned from this workbook, consider repeating them twice more or purchasing similar workbooks from the same author.

If you were to ask Dani what her thoughts are about CBT, she would tell you how much it has helped her solve all sorts of sticky situations in her life, ranging from tackling school assignments to expressing big emotions with clarity and confidence.

With practice, you will also have positive things to say about this type of therapy and the different skills it has taught you on how to confront difficult situations.

If you have enjoyed completing this workbook, please leave a review on the book's Amazon page!

About the Author

Richard Bass

Richard Bass is a well-established author with extensive knowledge and background on children's disabilities. Richard has also experienced first-hand many children and teens who deal with depression and anxiety. He enjoys researching techniques and ideas to better serve students, as well as providing guidance to parents on how to understand and lead their children to success.

Richard wants to share his experience, research, and practices through his writing, as it has proven successful for many parents and students.

Richard feels there is a need for parents and others around the child to fully understand the disability or the mental health of the child. He hopes that with his writing, people will be more understanding of children going through these issues.

Richard Bass has been in education for over a decade and holds a bachelor's and master's degree in education as well as several certifications, including Special Education K-12 and Educational Administration.

Whenever Richard is not working, reading, or writing, he likes to travel with his family to learn about different cultures and get ideas from all around about the upbringing of children, especially those with disabilities. In addition, Richard researches and learns about different educational systems around the world.

Richard participates in several online groups where parents, educators, doctors, and psychologist share their success with children with disabilities. Richard is in the process of growing a Facebook-Meta-group where further discussion about his books and techniques could take place.

Apart from online groups, he has also attended trainings regarding the upbringing of students with disabilities and led trainings in this area.

A Message from the Author

If you enjoyed the book and are interested on further updates or just a place to share your thoughts with other readers or myself, please join my Facebook group by scanning below!

If you would be interested on receiving a **FREE** Planner for kids **PDF** version, by signing up you will also receive exclusive notifications to when new content is released and will be able to receive it at a promotional price. Scan below to sign up!

Scan below to check out my content on YouTube and learn more about Neurodiversity!

References

Abrams, Z. (2023, January 1). Kid's mental health is in crisis. Here's what psychologists are doing to help. APA. https://www.apa.org/monitor/2023/01/trends-improving-youth-mental-health

Barkley, S. (2022, March 22). Why it's not a sign of weakness to ask for help? Power of Positivity. https://www.powerofpositivity.com/ask-for-help-not-weakness/

Barnes, M. J. (2023, May). Dealing with difficult emotions (for teens). KidsHealth. https://kidshealth.org/en/teens/stressful-feelings.html

Bennet, R. T. (2021, February 15). 66 Inspiring positive quotes for negative thinkers. Utterly Positive. https://utterlypositive.com/positive-quotes-for-negative-thinkers/

Bilodeau, K. (2021, October 1). Managing intrusive thoughts. Harvard Health. https://www.health.harvard.edu/mind-and-mood/managing-intrusive-thoughts#:~:text=It%20seems%20to%20come%20out

Burgunder, B. (n.d.). Brittany Burgunder quotes. Goodreads. https://www.goodreads.com/author/show/14671015.Brittany_Burgunder

d'Ath, K., & Willson, R. (2023, September 1). Best 35 CBT quotes (cognitive behavioral therapy). Ineffable Living. https://ineffableliving.com/cbt-quotes-cognitive-behavioral-therapy/

Danaher, M. (2023, June 27). The power of pausing to improve your life. LinkedIn. https://www.linkedin.com/pulse/power-pausing-improve-your-life-mark/

Deschene, L. (n.d.). Lori Deschene quotes. Goodreads. https://www.goodreads.com/author/show/5130095.Lori_Deschene

Emerson, R. W. (2015, October 15). Ten quotes that sum up CBT perfectly. Daniel Fryer. https://www.danielfryer.com/2015/10/15/ten-quotes-that-sum-up-cbt-perfectly/

Himani. (2023, January 31). Intrusive negative thoughts: examples, triggers and tips. Mantra Care. https://mantracare.org/ocd/ocd-symptoms/intrusive-negative-thoughts/

Hogan, L. (2021, August 25). How to be more empathetic. WebMD. https://www.webmd.com/balance/features/how-to-be-more-empathetic

Indeed Editorial Team. (2022, December 10). What is open communication? (With benefits and importance). Indeed Career Guide. https://www.indeed.com/career-advice/career-development/what-is-open-communication

Indeed Editorial Team. (2023, February 28). 14 Effective problem-solving strategies. Indeed Career Guide. https://www.indeed.com/career-advice/career-development/problem-solving-strategies

Jivanjee, P., Brennan, E., & Gonzalez-Prats, M. C. (2016). Building community supports for young people in the transition years: A tip sheet for service providers. In Pathways RTC. https://www.pathwaysrtc.pdx.edu/pdf/projPTTP-Community-Support-Tip-Sheet.pdf

Keller, H. (2020, January 27). 17 Powerfully effective quotes about purging negativity from your life once and for all. IncAfrica. https://incafrica.com/library/peter-economy-17-powerfully-effective-quotes-about-purging-negativity-from-your-life-once-for-all

Marcin, A. (2023, March 10). Cognitive behavioral therapy: How CBT works. Healthline. https://www.healthline.com/health/cognitive-behavioral-therapy#concepts

Relaxation techniques: Try these steps to reduce stress. (2022). Mayo Clinic. https://www.mayoclinic.org/healthy-lifestyle/stress-management/in-depth/relaxation-technique/art-20045368

Rich, T. (2019, April 3). Primary and secondary emotions. Richer Life Counseling. https://richerlifecounseling.com/primary-and-secondary-emotions/#:~:text=Primary%20emotions%20are%20the%20first

Robbins, A. (2019, May 8). 40 Team communication quotes to inspire your team. Tameday. https://www.tameday.com/team-communication-quotes/

Schwegman, K. (2022, January 7). Unhealthy communication habits to be aware of & how to respond. HolisticWellnessPractice. https://www.holisticwellnesspractice.com/hwp-blog/2022/01/07/unhealthy-communication-habits-to-be-aware-of-how-to-respond-instead

Seneca, L. A. (2015, October 15). Ten quotes that sum up CBT perfectly. Daniel Fryer. https://www.danielfryer.com/2015/10/15/ten-quotes-that-sum-up-cbt-perfectly/

South Pacific Private Hospital. (2022, May 2). Signs you're not coping. Marie Claire. https://www.marieclaire.com.au/signs-youre-not-coping

Stanborough, R. J. (2023, June 5). Cognitive restructuring: techniques and examples. Healthline. https://www.healthline.com/health/cognitive-restructuring

Tahir, S. (n.d.). Sabaa Tahir quotes. Goodreads. https://www.goodreads.com/author/show/7770873.Sabaa_Tahir

What is problem solving? Steps, process and techniques. (2021). ASQ. https://asq.org/quality-resources/problem-solving#:~:text=Problem%20solving%20is%20the%20act

Williams, B. (n.d.). Quotes about problem-solving. Great Expectations. https://www.greatexpectations.org/resources/life-principles/problem-solving/quotes-about-problem-solving/

Image References

Cameron, J. M. (2020a). Girl in pink and white shirt sitting beside brown wooden table [Image]. Pexels. https://www.pexels.com/photo/girl-in-pink-and-white-shirt-sitting-beside-brown-wooden-table-4143795/

Cameron, J. M. (2020b). Girl in pink shirt sitting on couch [Image]. Pexels. https://www.pexels.com/photo/girl-in-pink-shirt-sitting-on-couch-4144042/

Cameron, J. M. (2020c). Photo of girl writing on white paper [Image]. Pexels. https://www.pexels.com/photo/photo-of-girl-writing-on-white-paper-4143794/

Cameron, J. M. (2020d). Woman in pink crew neck t-shirt holding tablet computer [Image]. Pexels. https://www.pexels.com/photo/woman-in-pink-crew-neck-t-shirt-holding-tablet-computer-4144038/

Dinu, D. (2015). People watching concert photography [Image]. Pexels. https://www.pexels.com/photo/people-watching-concert-photography-849/

Fischer, M. (2020a). A teacher standing in the classroom [Image]. Pexels. https://www.pexels.com/photo/a-teacher-standing-in-the-classroom-5212703/

Fischer, M. (2020b). A two girls using laptop with classmates [Image]. Pexels. https://www.pexels.com/photo/a-two-girls-using-laptop-with-classmates-5212695/

Fischer, M. (2020c). Girl in blue long sleeve shirt and brown backpack [image]. Pexels. https://www.pexels.com/photo/girl-in-blue-long-sleeve-shirt-and-brown-backpack-5212322/

Fischer, M. (2020d). Group of students with their teacher [Image]. Pexels. https://www.pexels.com/photo/group-of-students-with-their-teacher-5212352/

Holmes, K. (2020). Crop pupils writing in copybook on desk [Image]. Pexels. https://www.pexels.com/photo/crop-pupils-writing-in-copybook-on-desk-5905959/

Made in United States
North Haven, CT
28 December 2023

46746331R00067